MW01255129

DIVINE ALLUREMENT

CRANMER'S COMFORTABLE WORDS

A lecture in honour of the Revd Dr Peter Toon

BY ASHLEY NULL

The Latimer Trust

Divine Allurement: Cranmer's Comfortable Words © Ashley Null 2014

ISBN   978-1-906327-23-1

Cover photo: © rck- fotolia.com

The Toon Lecture is administered by Church Society

Published by the Latimer Trust July 2014

The Latimer Trust (formerly Latimer House, Oxford) is a conservative Evangelical research organisation within the Church of England, whose main aim is to promote the history and theology of Anglicanism as understood by those in the Reformed tradition. Interested readers are welcome to consult its website for further details of its many activities.

The Latimer Trust
London N14 4PS UK
Registered Charity: 1084337
Company Number: 4104465
Web: www.latimertrust.org
E-mail: administrator@latimertrust.org

CONTENTS

Introduction

Peter Toon was a Yorkshireman, an Anglican clergyman, theologian, and church historian. Former librarian of Latimer House in Oxford, curate of St Ebbe's, and later a tutor at Oak Hill, after a brief spell in County Durham he was invited to become Professor of Philosophical and Systematic Theology at an Episcopal Seminary in Wisconsin, and served churches in the United States until almost the end of his life. He was for many years the President of the Prayer Book Society in the United States, but eventually returned to England to serve as Priest-in-Charge of a Staffordshire village church. He was widely in demand as a speaker throughout the Commonwealth, Europe, and Asia.

Dr. Toon died in April 2009. He left behind around 40 books and numerous essays and articles on a wide variety of topics from Puritanism and popular doctrinal works, to spirituality and liturgy. As well as editing *The Concise Evangelical Dictionary of Theology* and *The Compact Bible Dictionary*, he wrote on the great Puritan, John Owen, publishing his *Oxford Orations*, his surviving correspondence, and a biography, *God's Statesman*. But the burden of much of Peter Toon's writing was for the importance of the historic formularies of the Church of England: the *Thirty-nine Articles*, the *Book of Common Prayer*, and the Ordinal.

He also left his beloved wife of more than 48 years, Vita, and their daughter, Deborah, and it is with their help that a new annual lectureship – the Peter Toon Lecture – has been established, in the hope that it will contribute to the strengthening of God's church, and particularly the Reformed Catholic faith of the Church of England.

The annual lectureship is administered by Church Society and in 2014, the Revd Canon Dr Ashley Null delivered the following lecture as the opening event of the Church Society Conference, "Positively Anglican", at Oak Hill Theological College in London, following a service of Evensong according to the *Book of Common Prayer*. Our hope is that it will stimulate, edify, and inspire all who read it, as it did those who first heard it on that occasion, that they may be allured by the grace of the gospel of Christ to love and serve the Lord.

Revd Dr Lee Gatiss (Chairman of the organising committee)
Revd Dr Andrew Atherstone
Revd Dr Andrew Cinnamond
Mrs Vita Toon

Divine Allurement: Cranmer's Comfortable Words

A lecture in honour of the Revd Dr Peter Toon

One of the reformers' favorite verbs to use with the Gospel was 'allure'. According to the *Oxford English Dictionary*, the word comes from the practice in falconry of casting a meat-laden lure to recall a bird of prey. Such hawking was a pursuit for gentlemen and, thus, a common recreation amongst the people at the court of Henry VIII. Even Thomas Cranmer, the Archbishop of Canterbury, was a frequent falconer. He was well-known to find refreshment after long study through hawking, for his father had made sure that his son was practiced in the sport from youth as a sign of his good birth, despite their relatively modest means.[1]

Because justification by faith emphasized personal faith, persuasion was important to the Protestant Reformers. Hence, Martin Luther found 'allure' a useful word to describe how Christ wooed sinners back to himself:

> Thus, when the shepherd finds the lost sheep again, he has no intention of pushing it away in anger once more or throwing it to a hungry wolf. Rather, all his care and concern is directed to alluring it with every possible kindness. Treating it with the upmost tenderness, he takes the lamb upon his own back, lifting it up and carrying it, until he brings the animal all the way home again.[2]

For Luther such gentle handling was the key to people coming to personal faith: 'How very kindly and lovingly does the Lord allure all hearts to himself, and in this way he stirs them to believe in him.'[3]

Naturally, then, the early English Protestants also considered 'allure' an especially apt term for expressing their understanding of the

---

[1] John Gough Nichols, ed., *Narratives of the Days of the Reformation* (London: Camden Society, First Series, 77, 1859), p. 239.

[2] Martin Luther, *D. Martin Luthers Werke: Kritische Gesammtausgabe*, ed. J. K. F. Knaake, G. Kawerau, *et alia* (Weimar: Hermann Bohlaus Nachfolger, 1883-), vol 36 pp. 290-291.

[3] Luther, *D. Martin Luthers Werke*, vol 8, p. 359.

process of salvation. Firstly, conversion to the truth had to come from persuasive preaching, not just by proclamation and punishment. Richard Taverner used 'allure' to stress this point in his 1540 handbook of Sunday sermons:

> The Romish bishop erreth and doth naught in that he goeth about by violence to draw men to the Christian faith. For besides the preaching of the Gospel, Christ gave nothing in commission unto his disciples. So they preached it accordingly to their commission and left it in men's free liberty to come to it or not. They said not, either believe it or I will kill thee. So ye see that infidels as Turks, Saracens, and Jews ought not violently to be drawn to our faith, but lovingly rather invited and allured.[4]

Secondly, 'allure' as gentleness and kindness fit precisely with the English Reformers' understanding of salvation by grace. In his book of sermons for Holy Days, Taverner went on specifically to define forgiveness as what God used to draw people to himself: 'God freely pardoning all our sins doth allure us all, of whom he hath been offended, to peace and amity.'[5]

Thirdly, the sense of 'allure' included an appeal to the hearers' own inner longings. For the English Reformers, to encounter unconditional divine love was to discover something deep within being touched—an unquenchable, often unexpected, longing for a relationship with one's Maker being stirred up; a transforming grateful human love for God being gently drawn out; a fervent drive to express this love in all outward actions rising up and directing the remainder of their lives. Fear of punishment could not produce such an inward, all-encompassing transformation in a sinner. Only the assurance of divine love made known in free pardon had that power. Perhaps no one expressed the results of feeling the alluring nature of the Gospel better than Thomas Becon, Cranmer's chaplain.

> As I may unfeignedly report unto you the affect of my heart, verily since that ye declared to us the goodness of God the Father toward us through Jesus Christ I have felt in my heart such an earnest faith and burning love toward God and his

---

[4]   Richard Taverner, *The Epistles and Gospels with a Brief Postil upon the same from after Easter till Advent* (London: Richard Bankes, 1540), sig. 42v.

[5]   Richard Taverner, *On Saint Andrew's Day the Gospels with brief Sermons upon them for all the Holy Days in the Year* (London: Richard Bankes, 1542), fol. 49v.

Word, that me think a thousand fires could not pluck me away from the love of him. I begin now utterly to condemn, despise, reject, cast away, and set at naught all the pleasures of this world, wherein I have so greatly rejoiced in times past. All the threats of God, all the displeasures of God, all the fires and pains of hell could never before this day so allure me to the love of God, as you have now done by expressing unto me the exceeding mercy and unspeakable kindness of God toward us wretched sinners, insomuch that now from the very heart I desire to know what I may do, that by some means I may show again my heart to be full fired on the seeking of his glory. For I now desire nothing more than the advancement of his name.[6]

This good news of salvation by transforming grace alone was what Cranmer sought to sum up in one of his most famous compositions for the new English liturgy he devised – Holy Communion's Comfortable Words. Here is the Gospel according to Reformation Anglicanism.

Hear what comfortable words our Saviour Christ sayeth to all that truly turn to him. [7]

Cranmer's opening sentence highlighted the inter-connectedness of Gospel, comfort and Christ. It was, after all, an important point in dispute between Catholics and Protestants.

Walk into any medieval parish church and above the chancel arch was a painting of Jesus as Judge. It dominated the whole interior of the nave. There on high before every parishioner's eyes Christ sat in judgment at the general resurrection, sending some people to the devils in Hell, while sending others to be welcomed by angelic choirs into Heaven. Here was the high point of a 'moralistic strain' in late medieval piety which Eamon Duffy himself admitted 'could be oppressive':

Churches contained not only the chancel-arch representation of the Day of Doom, with its threat of terrifying reckoning down to

---

[6] Thomas Becon, *A Christmas Banquet Garnished with Many Pleasant and Dainty Dishes* (John Mayler for John Gough, 1542), sigs. F4v-5r.

[7] Cranmer's Comfortable Words here are as found in the 1549 and 1552 *Book of Communion Prayer*, see Joseph Ketley, ed., *The Two Liturgies ... in the reign of King Edward the Sixth* (Cambridge: Cambridge University Press for the Parker Society, 1844), pp. 92, 276.

the last farthing, but wall-paintings and windows illustrating the deadly sins, the works of mercy, the Commandments, Christ wounded by sabbath-breaking, the figures of the three living and the three dead, or the related *danse macabre*.[8]

Indeed, according to Duffy, the 'whole machinery of late medieval piety was designed to shield the soul from Christ's doomsday anger'.[9] Little wonder Duffy had to admit again that the omnipresent threat of terror 'must have seemed at times oppressive'. The English reformers, however, rejected such a proclamation of the Gospel as 'bad news'. They wanted the English people to know that Christ was first and foremost the Good Shepherd who allured his lost sheep back by the power of his self-sacrificing love.

Naturally, then, Cranmer's Comfortable Words do not begin with God's wrath. In fact, they do not start with God at all. Rather, the first Scripture verse focuses on hurting humanity–with its felt needs, its longing for wholeness. The Comfortable Words begin with Matthew 11:28:

Come unto to me all that travail, and be heavy laden, and I shall refresh you.

Human misery caused by captivity to the destructive power of sin was a favorite theme of the English Reformers. They wholeheartedly agreed with Luther's teaching that the human heart cannot, of itself, free itself from slavery to sin and selfishness. Listen to what the second sermon from the *Book of Homilies* says. Entitled 'The Misery of All Mankind', it concisely sums up sin's effect on human nature: 'We are sheep that run astray, but we cannot of our own power come again to the sheepfold, so great is our imperfection and weakness.'[10] In fact, Cranmer appears to have chosen the word 'travail' instead of the more usual 'labour' specifically because of its inclusion of emotional, not

---

[8]   Eamon Duffy, *The Stripping of the Altars: Traditional Religion in England c. 1400-c. 1580* (London: Yale University Press, 1992), p. 187.
[9]   Duffy, *The Stripping of the Altars*, p. 309.
[10]   Ronald B. Bond, ed., *Certain Sermons or Homilies (1547) AND A Homily against Disobedience and Wilful Rebellion (1570): A Critical Edition* (Toronto: University of Toronto Press, 1987), p. 74.

merely physical, weariness."[11]   He gave an enduring voice to the *Anfechtungen* (spiritual anxieties) of the sin-sick soul in his prayer of confession for Communion in the 1549 *Book of Common Prayer*:

> Almighty God, Father of our Lord Jesus Christ, maker of all things, judge of all men, we acknowledge and bewail our manifold sins and wickedness . . . the remembrance of them is grievous unto us, the burden of them is intolerable.

Slavery to act out in selfishness, and the innate sense of guilt which resulted – here were the two fundamental sources for human misery. What could be done about them? For the English Reformers, the answer lay in divine action alone.   We can see this in the absolution which followed the confession.   The minister asked God to 'pardon and deliver' the congregation. Why two verbs instead of merely one? Because Cranmer was making clear that humanity needed to turn to God as the only antidote for both sources of human misery. Only God could heal a conscience wounded by selfish acts.[12] Only God could draw to his purposes a will chained to self-centredness.

In the 1552 prayer book, Cranmer reinforced these themes by adding a new opening for the Daily Office which once again compared sin-sodden humanity to helpless sheep:

> Almighty and most merciful Father, we have erred and strayed from thy ways, like lost sheep. We have followed too much the devices and desires of our own hearts. We have offended against thy holy laws. We have left undone those things which we ought to have done, and we have done those things which we ought not to have done, and there is no health in us.[13]

Now both Morning and Evening Prayer began with a confession of humanity's profound spiritual neediness in the face of its on-going struggle with self-centred waywardness.   As a result, Cranmer made the

---

[11] Whereas Tyndale's *New Testament*, the Henrician Primers (see, e.g., *A Primer in English* (London: John Byddell, 1534), sig. L3v) and the Great Bible use 'labour', Erasmus wrote: 'Come unto me (sayeth he) as many of you as be grieved with afflictions, cares, or with conscience of your sins, and as many as be oppressed with the burden of adversity, I will refresh you, I will give you solace and comfort against all kinds of displeasures', Erasmus, *The First Volume of the Paraphrase of Erasmus upon the New Testament* (London: Edward Whitchurch,1548), fol. 70r.
[12] Ketley, *Liturgies of Edward VI*, pp. 6-7, 90-1.
[13] Ketley, *Liturgies of Edward VI*, pp. 218-19.

essence of Anglican worship to be turning to God because of sin, so as to be turned by God from it.

So God loved the world, that he gave his only begotten Son to the end that all that believe in him, should not perish, but have life everlasting.

Having used Jesus' own words to acknowledge the depth of human longing for good news, Cranmer's second Comfortable Word now turns again to Jesus to establish the depth of God's own longing to respond. The divine desire and initiative to save his people is at the very heart of the English Reformers' theology. John 3:16 makes clear that God the Father, moved by the love which is his very being, sent God the Son into this world to become the visible embodiment of the divine Good Shepherd. Jesus came to seek out the lost, gently freeing lambs caught in the thicket of sin. He laid down his own life so that in the end he could bear his wandering creatures safely back to the flock on his own wounded shoulders. In the face of such alluring love, the Reformers were convinced that humanity could not but be drawn out of their deeply entrenched soul-sickness back to their Creator by the stirring up of their own inner longings.

Of course, the medieval church read John 3:16 as well. In fact, the typical English depiction of Jesus as coming Judge had him displaying his wounds and the instruments of the torture he suffered on their behalf.[14] Yet this depiction of divine love was not intended to be a means of wooing humanity back to the fold. Rather, the reminder of Christ's passion was to render them without excuse if they had failed to repent. In effect, the medieval church said to Christians, 'Here, look at what Jesus did for you. What have you done for him lately?' Because of that 'moralistic strain' noted by Duffy, the medieval church expected Christians to sweat to prove themselves worthy of the divine love which had been so costly lavished on them.

Nothing could have been further from the Reformers' understanding. Here is the truly revolutionary nature of the Gospel they found in Scripture. The red thread that runs throughout Cranmer's writings is this simple truth: The glory of God is to love the unworthy. For the early English Protestants, nothing established that principle as clearly as God's decision not to base salvation on personal merit, not

---

[14]   Duffy, *Stripping of the Altars*, p. 157.

even on the kind of grace-assisted human choices that the King's Book insisted was the true interpretation of Augustine.[15] No, personal belief brought about salvation, as John 3:16 suggested, rather than personal accomplishment. Eternal life with God came through simply trusting his saving acts on humanity's behalf, rather than one's own. In short, by faith sinners were adopted into God's family forever. They no longer had to fear that they were merely foster children who had to live under the constant threat of being disowned as the Devil's in the face of every fresh case of disobedience.

Hear also what Saint Paul sayeth.
This is a true saying, and worthy of all men to be received, that Jesus Christ came into the world to save sinners.

Having laid out the two sides – the longing of humanity for relief and the longing of God to rescue – Cranmer's third Comfortable Word circles back like a hawk to the human condition, but now at a higher level. On the one hand, humanity's situation is no longer described in subjective terms of felt needs but rather as the objective consequences of violating divine law. Humanity suffers from spiritual fatigue because that is merely the most readily apparent fruit of human sinfulness. As rebels against divine order, they are cut off from God's peace now and stand under the threat of the divine wrath to come. Humanity's refreshment can only come by addressing humanity's sin. On the other hand, to do so is also clearly beyond human beings. Having been so weakened by sin's power, humanity cannot co-operate with grace to achieve their salvation. According to Cranmer, that would be the 'ready way unto desperation'.[16] 1 Timothy 1:15 makes plain that here is the reason Jesus came into this world. It is Christ's mission to save sinners, not their own. As Cranmer's 'Homily of Salvation' expressed it:

> Justification is not the office of man, but of God. For man cannot justify himself by his own works neither in part nor in the whole . . . But justification is the office of God only, and is not a thing which we render unto him, but which we receive of him, not which we give to him, but which we take of him, by his

---

[15] T. A. Lacey, *The King's Book* (London: SPCK, 1932), pp. 147-151, and for the comment about Augustine, p. 149.

[16] J. E. Cox, *Miscellaneous Writings and Letters of Thomas Cranmer* (Cambridge: Cambridge University Press for the Parker Society, 1846), p. 94.

free mercy, and by the only merits of his most dearly beloved Son.[17]

Only upon realizing this distinction did Cranmer believe the English people could find refreshment from their spiritual fatigue.

Hear also what Saint John sayeth.
If any man sin, we have an advocate with the father, Jesus Christ the righteous, and he is the propitiation for our sins.

With the fourth Comfortable Word we have come full circle.   In I Timothy 1:15, the Gospel truth about the human condition was seen from the human point of view, i.e., 'How can I be saved?'. Now we turn to the Gospel truth about the human condition from God's perspective, i.e., 'How can God be true to both his righteous nature and his enduring love for an unrighteous humanity?'. I John 2:1-2 concisely states that problem from heaven's point-of-view. God's justice requires 'propitiation', i.e., the fulfilling of his determination to destroy sin because of all the hurt and harm it causes.   Of course, Cranmer's confession for Communion explicitly acknowledged the need for such propitiation, saying that the congregation had sinned 'by thought, word, and deed, against thy divine majesty, provoking most justly thy wrath and indignation against us'.[18]   That's why the only answer to human misery was utter divine graciousness, God's taking humanity's sin upon himself, so he could destroy sin on the cross without having to destroy humanity as well. Cranmer's Eucharistic prayer clearly affirmed the complete effectiveness of Christ's death to take away God's wrath. The cross was 'a full, perfect and sufficient sacrifice, oblation and satisfaction, for the sins of the whole world'.[19] As a result, according to the 'Homily on Salvation', 'the justice of God and his mercy did embrace together, and fulfilled the mystery of our redemption'.[20] What good news! As I John 2:1-2 reminds us, because Christ has made the sacrifice which has removed God's wrath from us, he now is our advocate. Jesus himself is the one who stands by our side. He is the one who answers for us when we are accused of being sinners! Here is the heart of the revolution in the understanding of Jesus that the English

---

[17]   Cox, *Cranmer's Miscellaneous Writings*, p. 131.
[18]   Ketley, *Liturgies of Edward VI*, pp. 91, 276.
[19]   Ketley, *Liturgies of Edward VI*, pp. 88, 279.
[20]   Cox, *Cranmer's Miscellaneous Writings*, p. 129.

Reformers wanted to proclaim. For believers, Jesus is not our judge. He is our defense lawyer.

Yet, there is still more to the story. John's use of legal language reinforced the Reformers' understanding of how people can have a right relationship with God. The theological term for that is 'justification', i.e., 'just as if I had never sinned, but always did God's will so as to live a life of perfect righteousness'. Protestants believe that this theological word should be understood in the legal sense of being 'declared righteous'. That's what 'justification' means in Greek, where δικαίωσις (dikaiōsis) is used specifically of what a judge does in a courtroom, acquitting defendants of charges by declaring them 'not guilty'. Of course, the medieval church used Latin, and in Latin 'justification' means 'to be made righteous'. That's why the medieval church argued that the moment someone had sinned, they no longer had a relationship with God. In the medieval view, only the perfectly righteous were 'justified', i.e., were good enough to have a relationship with God. Once they sinned, they lost their salvation until they did penance to become pure enough again to be acceptable to God.

Now the New Testament was written in Greek, so it made perfect sense to the English Reformers to follow the Greek understanding of the word rather than the later Latin one. Consequently, for Protestants, believers can have an on-going relationship with God, even though we are not totally freed from sin and selfishness in this life. When we trust Jesus to win divine forgiveness for us, he will act as our advocate. He will present the cross as the answer to the charges that we are not good enough for God. Then God the Father, as judge, will accept Jesus' righteousness as the best possible and indeed the only possible defense on our behalf. As Cranmer's confession for Holy Communion expressed it: 'for thy Son our Lord Jesus Christ's sake, forgive us all that is past.'[21] Because of Jesus, God the Father declares us 'not guilty' of any sin which would separate us from him. Thus, Cranmer concluded his four promises of the Gospel as he had begun, with utter reliance on Christ's saving activity both to meet human needs and to fulfill divine desires.

---

[21] Ketley, *Liturgies of Edward VI*, p. 91.

Lift up Your Hearts

With Cranmer's four Comfortable Words we have Reformation Anglicanism's Gospel of transforming grace. Here is his understanding of apostolic succession. Cranmer did not believe that the apostles passed down the Holy Spirit through an unbroken line of holy bishops like a pipeline. No, for Cranmer, the author of the founding formularies of Anglicanism, apostolic succession meant the passing down of apostolic teaching. Christian faith and morals had been divinely revealed and recorded in the Bible. Its saving truths were unalterable. Each generation of the church was to receive, witness to and pass on the Bible and its message of salvation by grace alone through faith alone. As each generation proclaimed this timeless Gospel through Word and Sacrament, the Holy Spirit would go forth afresh into the lives of that era, changing hearts, moving wills, and inspiring people to love and serve God and their neighbours.

If the message of transforming grace was to be unchanging, what about the packaging? As a Renaissance humanist like Erasmus, Cranmer believed every presentation of a message had to be tailored to the needs of its specific audience. How else could the audience be allured to embrace the message, unless the manner of the presentation took into account what would move them? Consequently, Cranmer taught that the church's presentation of the Gospel had to evolve and change as the society it addressed did. If the church didn't, how could it have any hope of continuing to reach its audience generation after generation? Liturgy had to proclaim the good news in the light of the current needs and aspirations of the people. In short, for Cranmer the Gospel message had to be unchanging, but its presentation equally had to be constantly adapting.

Of course we have already seen this missionary strategy at work. If the medieval English Church presented Jesus as a keen-eyed hawk scanning the flock to be sure to punish the slightest sin, Protestant preachers first had to seek to allure their people back to God with the good news of Jesus' genuine, gentle concern for humanity's own inner longings. Only then could they begin to lead their congregations gradually to greater doctrinal understanding. Clearly, all these themes came together in Cranmer's Comfortable Words. Nevertheless, they found their fullest expression in Cranmer's final placement of them at the very center of the church's greatest form of divine allurement – Holy Communion.

In keeping with his understanding of apostolic succession, Cranmer's 'Homily on Scripture' plainly taught that the Bible was a divine instrument by which God turned his people to himself: 'The words of Holy Scripture ... have power to convert through God's promise, and they be effectual through God's assistance ... they have ever a heavenly spiritual working in them.'[22] In the 1552 version of his Communion service, Cranmer decided to make the fresh proclamation of the Gospel the immediate supernatural means by which God drew his people towards a direct encounter with Him in the sacrament. When on trial for his life because of his views of the Eucharist, Cranmer made clear that he took literally the priest saying, 'Lift up your hearts!':

> We should consider, not what the bread and wine be in their own nature, but what they import to us and signify ... that lifting up our minds, we should look up to the blood of Christ with our faith, should touch him with our mind, and receive him with our inward man; and that, being like eagles in this life, we should fly up into heaven in our hearts, where that Lamb is resident at the right hand of his Father ... by whose passion we are filled at his table.[23]

Consequently, he revised the liturgy so that the minister said the four Gospel sentences immediately before asking the people to lift up their hearts. Now the Comfortable Words became God's divine instrument to allure believers to seek union with Christ and each other in heavenly places.

Finally, we can see the full scope of Cranmer's Gospel falconry which he tethered to the very heart of Anglican worship and, hence, its identity. In the 1552 *Book of Common Prayer*, Cranmer sent out Scripture's Comfortable Words, not so much as an eagle, but as a falcon, flying forth in a spiraling gyre, grounded in the human condition but gradually looping higher and higher towards the glory of the divine, holding humanity and the Trinity together in a dynamic mutual dialectic, funneling love from above into the hearts of the beloved below so that they at last have the power to love God and one another on earth as it is in Heaven.

---

[22] Bond, *Homilies*, p. 62.
[23] Cox, *Cranmer on the Lord's Supper*, p. 398.

On the massive dark oak organ screen which divides in two the chapel of King's College, Cambridge, amidst its numerous carved royal emblems of Henry VIII are examples of a crowned falcon sitting on a stump – the symbol for Anne Boleyn, Henry's wife at the time of the screen's construction. The same badge can be seen embossed on the ceiling of an inner gateway of Hampton Court Palace as well as high up in its Great Hall. Few today recognize these rare heraldic references to the brief reign of Queen Anne, architectural survivors of Henry's order to have all such reminders removed like his wife. Of course, with each ensuing decade of the Twenty-First Century, fewer and fewer Anglicans are familiar with Cranmer's falcon, for the continuing presence of the Comfortable Words in modern Anglican liturgies is as scant and scattered as the Boleyn badge. Yet, if Anne's falcon reminds us that Cranmer lived in turbulent times, too, then the Comfortable Words give us his answer, for when 'things fall apart; the centre cannot hold.'[24] This falcon is itself the lure, leading earthly eyes and hearts to look to and long for heavenly places. Today's falconers would do well to listen.

Ashley Null

---

[24] William Bulter Yeats, 'The Second Coming' in *The Collected Poems of W.B. Yeats* (Ware: Wordsworth Editions, 1994), p. 158.

The Writings of Peter Toon

With thanks to David Virtue of VirtueOnline (http://www.virtueonline.org), here is a list of Peter Toon's major publications.

His first piece appeared in *The Baptist Quarterly* (a publication of the Baptist Union of Great Britain) on the topic of 'The Strict and Particular Baptists' in 1963 when he was studying for the B.D. at King's College, University of London.

His first book continued the theme of 'Calvinism' and appeared in 1967 as *The Emergence of Hyper-Calvinism in English Nonconformity, 1689-1765*. It has a Preface by Dr. J. I. Packer and it was the cause of various invitations to the author to lecture in the U.S.A.

Then, in general categories, his works may be listed thus:

On English Puritanism
The Emergence of Hyper-Calvinism (1967)
The Correspondence of John Owen (1970)
Puritans the Millennium (1970)
Puritans and Calvinism (1971)
God's Statesman (1972)
The University Orations of Dr John Owen (1973)

Semi-Popular Doctrinal Writings
El Dios Siempre Presente
The Right of Private Judgment (1975)
Jesus Christ is Lord (1978)
Free to Obey (1979)
God Here and Now (1979)
God's Church for Today (1980)
God's Kingdom for Today (1980)
God's Salvation for Today (1980)
Protestant and Catholic (1983)
What's the Difference? (1983)
What We Believe (1984)
Your Conscience as Your Guide (1984)
General Godliness and True Piety (2000)

Serious Doctrinal Writing
Justification and Sanctification (1983)
The Ascension of our Lord (1984)
Heaven and Hell (1986)
The End of Liberal Theology (1995)

Yesterday, Today and Forever (1996)
Our Triune God (1996 & 2002)

On Spirituality
About Turn: the Decisional Event of Conversion (1987)
Born Again (1987)
What is Spirituality? (1989)
Spiritual Companions (100?)

Meditation
From Mind to Heart (1987)
Longing for Heaven (1987)
Meditating as a Christian (1991)
The Art of Meditating on Scripture (1993)
Meditating Upon God's Word (1998)

On Anglican Theology and Liturgy
The Ordinal and its Revision (1974)
The Development of Doctrine in the Church (1979)
Evangelical Theology 1833-1856 (1979)
The Anglican Way, Evangelical and Catholic (1983)
Britain's True Greatness (1984)
Let Women be Women (1990)
Knowing God through the Liturgy (1992)
Proclaiming the Gospel through the Liturgy (1993)
Which Rite is Right? (1994)
Common Worship Considered (2003)
Reforming Forwards? (2003)
The Order for Evening Prayer (1662) Annotated (2004)
The Order for Holy Communion (1662) Annotated (2004)
The Order for Holy Communion (1928) Annotated (2004)
Same-Sex Affection, Holiness and Ordination (2005)
Worship Without Dumbing Down (2005)
The Anglican Formularies and Holy Scripture (2006)
Anglican Identity (2006)
Episcopal Innovations 1960-2004 in ECUSA (2006)
Mystical Washing and Spiritual Regeneration (2007)
On Salvation and the Church of Rome – Richard Hooker (2007)

Writings in cooperation with Lou Tarsitano, edited by Toon
The Way, The Truth and the Life: The Anglican Walk (1998)
Dear Primates (2000)
Neither Archaic nor Obsolete (2003)
Neither Orthodoxy nor a Formulary (2004)

Essays with others in Books edited by Toon wholly or partly
Puritans, the Millennium and the Future of Israel (1970)
John Charles Ryle, Evangelical Bishop (1976)
One God in Trinity (1980)
Real Questions (with David Field, 1982)
Let God be God (1990)
A Guidebook to the Spiritual Life (1998)

Individual Essays in Books edited by others
"Anglicanism in Popish Dress," in *Tradition Renewed* (1986)
"Appreciating Mary Today" in *Chosen by God, Mary* (1989)
"The Articles and Homilies" in *The Study of Anglicanism* (1998)
Chaps 2 & 3 in *To Mend the Net* (2001)
"Episcopalianism" in *Who Runs The Church?* (2004)
"Justification by Faith Alone" in *Justification and Sanctification* (Canada 2008)

Dictionaries as an Editor
The Compact Bible Dictionary (1987)
NIV Bible Guide (1987)
The Concise Dictionary of the Christian Tradition (1989)
The Concise Evangelical Dictionary of Theology (1992)

Prayer Books as primary editor
Worshipping the Lord in the Anglican Way (2004)
An Anglican Prayer Book (2008)

Classic short works on the Devotional Life as editor
St Francis de Sales, Introduction to the Devout Life (1988)
Christ for All Seasons, Thomas a Kempis (1989)
Benjamin Jenks, Prayers for Families (1990)

Magazines edited by the author
HOME WORDS, Parish magazine insert C of E, 1985-
MANDATE, Prayer Book Society Magazine, USA, 1995-2008

If you have enjoyed this book, you might like to consider

- *supporting the work of the Latimer Trust*
- *reading more of our publications*
- *recommending them to others*

See www.latimertrust.org for more information.

Latimer Publications

CPSIA information can be obtained at www.ICGtesting.com
Printed in the USA
LVOW11s1203181014

409422LV00002B/35/P